Everyone Farts
It's OK to pass gas!

Story by:

P.B. Jelly

Illustrated by:

Md. Monoar Hossain Shaikat

Copyright © 2014

Copyright © 2014

All rights Reserved. No part of this publication or the information in it may be quoted from or reproduced in any form by means such as printing, scanning, photocopying or otherwise without prior written permission of the copyright holder.

For Ryan

EVERYONE FARTS AS YOU WILL SOON SEE,
A HIPPO FARTS..................

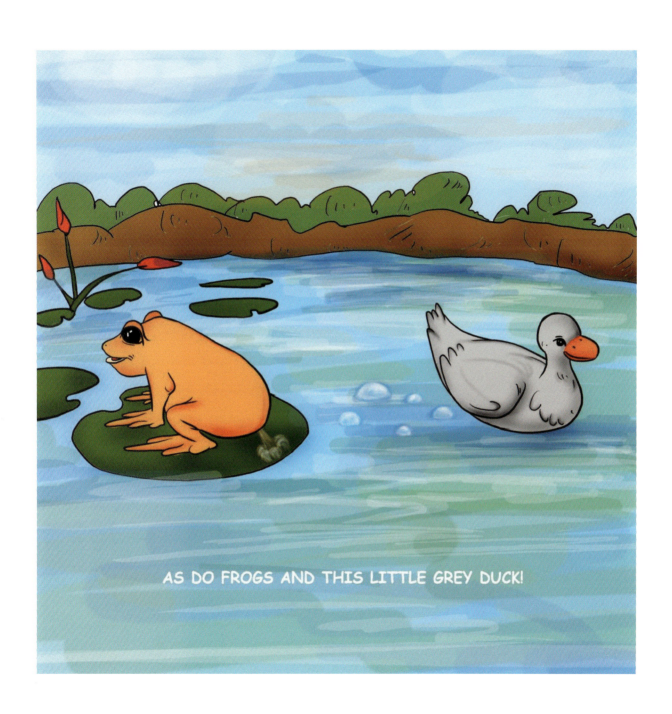
AS DO FROGS AND THIS LITTLE GREY DUCK!

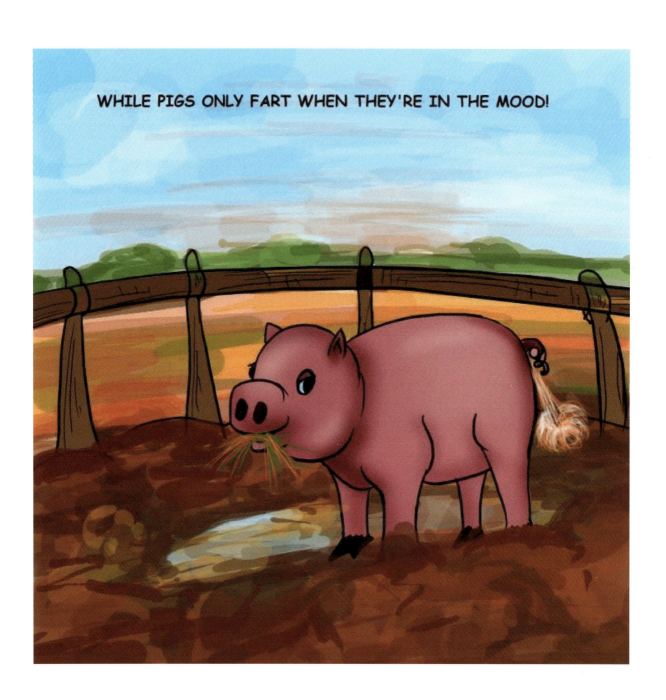

Thank you so much for reading my book! I hope you had as much fun reading it as I did writing it.

P.B. Jelly

CPSIA information can be obtained at www.ICGtesting.com
Printed in the USA
LVIW01n1007181017
552869LV00002B/10